WALTHAMSTOW

IN THE EARLY

NINETEENTH CENTURY

By

RICHARD S. SMITH

P R 1. 7 1. 1.8 1. L A

©Walthamstow Antiquarian Society
Vestry House Museum, Vestry Road, London E17 9NH
Monograph (New Series) No. 24

First published 1938
This edition 1981

ISBN 0 85480 040 9

Cover illustration: St. Peter's Church, Woodford New Road,
built 1840 to the design of John Shaw, Jnr. (Vestry House Museum).

Back cover: Walthamstow Token minted at the Coppermill in 1813.

The following paper was prepared originally to be read at a meeting of the Walthamstow Antiquarian Society, and makes no claim to a complete treatment. Such a treatment would necessitate a whole volume. Moreover, different aspects of the history of the parish in this period (*e.g.*, the story of the Walthamstow Houses and their occupants) have already been fully treated in the Society's Monographs.

What I have attempted is to give a fairly complete outline of the subject, to fill in the gaps in the existing printed material, and to indicate where information on other aspects of the local history of the period may be found.

RICHARD S. SMITH

WALTHAMSTOW MUSEUM,

September, 1938

Richard Smith was the first assistant curator at Vestry House Museum, and this new edition of his account is published to mark the 50th anniversary of the opening of the museum in 1931. The author is now retired and lives in Nottingham. The illustrations are new to the book; nos. 1 to 4 from the museum collection and the rest from my own.

W. G. S. Tonkin

ABBREVIATIONS

P.R.   Parochial Records (Walthamstow Museum).

W.C.   Walthamstow Collection (Walthamstow Museum).
         This is a collection of newspaper cuttings, etc.,
         formed by Mr. G. E. Roebuck some years ago.

E.C   Exhibition Collection (Walthamstow Museum).

W.A.S.   Walthamstow Antiquarian Society Monograph.

The reference numbers in the footnotes for the local collection have
been superseded by a new system, but the documents are still available.

WALTHAMSTOW
IN THE EARLY
NINETEENTH CENTURY

THE early nineteenth century is a period of crucial importance in English history. The rise of the industrial system which those years witnessed has an interest not merely for Britain, but for the whole world which has been transformed by that system. It is unnecessary to examine in any detail those influences which were changing England so drastically at this time. It will be sufficient to remember that certain developments in manufacture and agriculture were made just before and during this period—developments which themselves corresponded to the needs felt by the trade and industry which were growing up and preparing for further advances.

The main developments which characterise this transition period have been summarised as follows :—First, inventions in textile machinery leading to a great expansion in the cotton industry ; secondly, developments in the iron industry based on the smelting of iron with coal instead of charcoal ; and thirdly, the improvement of the steam engine.[1] These were the basic technological advances which were the root causes of the great changes in industry, transport, population, and social structure, and even ultimately of the changes in the spirit of the age, its literature and its arts.

---

[1] M. Dorothy George, *England in Transition* (1931), p. 143.

The immediate results of the Industrial Revolution must be well known to all, and it is only necessary to recall those which must be borne in mind when considering the story of Walthamstow during this period. Perhaps the most obvious was the tremendous increase in the possibilities of wealth production, and the enrichment of a section of the population. But side by side with this enrichment went the poverty and hardships of those men, women and children taken from their own little crafts and their traditional life on the land to work in the new factories.

Together with the increase in the possibilities of wealth production went, inevitably, an increase in the population. Walthamstow was not immediately affected by the growth of the big towns during the Industrial Revolution which transformed the Midlands and the North, except insofar as it was affected by the growth of London during this period. But Walthamstow inevitably felt the effect of the steep increase in population and the other changes which accompanied the Industrial Revolution. The antiquation of the old machinery of local government, the change in the position of agricultural labourers, educational and humanitarian developments—all have their reflection here and will be dealt with later on.

These, then, were the basic changes ushering in a new epoch in our history. But to fix the period in our minds, we must remember that it saw the wars against Napoleon, the last years of George III., the reigns of George IV. and William IV., and the accession of Queen Victoria. It saw the last flowering of Georgian taste in the stately dresses and houses of the Regency period, and it saw the grim new towns with houses huddled back-to-back in which lived a desperate population chained to the new steam-powered machinery. It witnessed the antics of the Regency Bucks on the one hand, and the beginnings of Trades Unions, the Luddite Riots and the Combination Acts on the other. It was the age of the stage coach and the quadrille, and of the beginnings of railways and gas-lighting. It was the age of John Nash, Keats, Words-worth and Shelley; the age, too, of cock-fighting and public executions for petty crimes. But perhaps we shall get the flavour of the period best if we recall the early novels of Charles Dickens, who grew to maturity in this turbulent period.

Although, as has been said, Walthamstow fortunately lay outside the area of industrialisation, one industry was established here in the early years of the nineteenth century which has an especial interest. The establish-ment of the Copper Rolling Mills on the Walthamstow Marshes gives this parish a direct link with the great industrial developments in other parts of the country.

We are indebted to the careful work of Mr. J. Coxall for the elucidation of the history of these mills.[1] The buildings which came to be occupied for work on copper had already had an interesting history, but unfortunately that history is not known to us in any detail. The Mills had been used for powder grinding in the seventeenth century, and for crushing linseed in the eighteenth; but towards the end of the seventeenth century there is frequent reference in the Parish Registers to the " Paper Mill on the Marshes,"[2] which indicates, I believe, yet another use to which the Mills have been put.

---

[1] J. Coxall, *The Walthamstow Tokens* (W.A.S. 18).
[2] See Baptismal Entries for 11 April, 1653, and 24 November, 1678, Walthamstow Parish Registers, Vol. 1.

The Mills were purchased by the British Copper Company probably in the year 1809. This company was one of many active in exploiting the mineral wealth of South Wales, and in 1807, the year of its foundation, erected its smelting works at Landore, a hamlet near Swansea. Shortly after the Walthamstow Mills were acquired, and employed in the rolling of copper ingots which were carried in barges from Swansea by sea, and thence up the River Lea. The power at the Mills was supplied by a stream of water diverted from the river, but when the Mills finally ceased working in 1857, we are told that a large boiler was taken away in three sections. This may mean that subsequently a steam engine had been installed. All the machinery was dismantled at this date, and removed in barges to the Morfa Rolling Mills at Swansea. It would be interesting to know whether any of this primitive machinery still exists today. Soon afterwards, what remained of the old buildings was taken over by the East London Waterworks Company, and Walthamstow people must be familiar with the pleasant old buildings which can be seen from the railway beyond the reservoirs. Before the Mills ceased, the industry had given its name to Copper Mill Lane. Previously, the road from the Marshes to Hoe Street had been known as Marsh Street along all its length.

The range of Walthamstow Tokens produced by the British Copper Company cover the years 1809 to 1814. These tokens, which circulated so widely, were not made in Walthamstow, but were produced elsewhere from copper rolled at the Mills. They have been exhaustively studied,[1] and nearly every variety is included in a

---

[1] J. Coxall (W.A.S. 18).

collection which Mr. Coxall has recently presented to the Walthamstow Museum. But very little is known of the processes employed, or of the people who worked at the Copper Mills. The only information available seems to be that provided by the Parish Registers. In their pages are references to coppersmiths, copper-forgers, copper-refiners, and copper-rollers, which would seem to indicate that the scope of the Mills was somewhat wider than has generally been considered. All these men lived either at the Copper Mills, or else in Marsh Street, conveniently close to their work.

The industry at the Copper Mills has been dealt with at some length because its establishment in the parish was the most obvious and direct result of the Industrial Revolution. Perhaps the next most obvious result was the increase of population here. The census returns for Walthamstow for 1811, 1821 and 1831[1] reveal some very interesting facts.

The 1811 census records that in 1801, 515 inhabited houses sheltered 599 families, comprising a total population of 3,006, which was made up of 1,413 males and 1,593 females. In 1811 we find 555 inhabited houses, 638 families, 1,771 males, 2,006 females, making a total population of 3,777—an increase of 26 per cent. Richard Abbey, who was Overseer at the time, was requested to account for "the Cause of the Difference in the Population of this Parish between the Years 1801 and 1811," and puts his finger on the right causes in his reply, "The increase of population as per the preceding account I attribute to the General prosperity of the Country, excepting the Establishment of two large Schools and a

---

[1] These census returns are in the P.R. collection.

9

Copper Mill containing together 159 persons since 1801."
The two large schools which had been established since
1801 appear to have been Cogan's Academy, which
returns 48 males and 11 females, and another school run
by a Stephen Eardley[1] which seems to have been twice
as large as Cogan's, with 85 males and 9 females. From
the 1811 Rate Book[2] we find that this school was situated
at Whipps Cross.

The analysis in the 1811 returns of the way in which
the families were employed is interesting. 220 families
were employed in Agriculture, 253 in Trade, Manufacture
or Handicraft, and 165 in other occupations. Agriculture, then, was quite obviously the main industry, but
Abbey adds this illuminating note to these figures:
" I have found it impossible to class the principal employ-
ment of Families with any precision on account of many
of the poor families being employed sometimes in
Agriculture, and sometimes as assistants in other em-
ployment." This drift from the land, and the inability of
agricultural labourers to get a living from the land all the
year round, was symptomatic of the times, and will be
dealt with later.

In the 1821 census returns, a further substantial increase in the population is recorded, the figure being
4,304, an increase of 14 per cent. on the 1811 figure.
The number of inhabited houses increased from 555 to
675, and the number of families inhabiting them from
638 to 845. But significantly, whilst the number of
families employed in Trade, Manufacture and Handicraft
had doubled in the ten years from 1811 to 1821, increas-

---

[1] This school was known as Paradise House Academy. W.C. 800.
[2] P.R. 174.

10

ing from 253 to 498, the number of families employed in Agriculture in 1821 appears as almost exactly half the number returned for 1811, dropping from 220 to 115.

There are no detailed analyses of the figures for the next few decades in the Parochial Records, but for the next 30 years the population remained almost stationary. In 1831 the figure had dropped slightly to 4,258, in 1841 it stood at 4,873, and in 1851 at 4,959. I believe the reason to be that these country districts in the vicinity of London shared in the general increase in population resulting from the Industrial Revolution largely in the shape of an influx of new merchant families with their train of servants, and once this influx had abated, there was no reason for further increase until improved transport facilities brought residence in Walthamstow within reach of other sections of the population.[1] But though population remained stationary here between 1820 and 1850, we must remember that in the industrial areas and in London, population continued to increase. The areas immediately around London were soon fairly well absorbed by its growth,[2] and the increase of population after 1850 in Walthamstow indicates that the tide of London's expansion had reached Walthamstow, and the process had begun which was to culminate in the complete transformation of the old village of Walthamstow.

For any detailed information as to the occupations of our population in the early nineteenth century, it is

---

[1] The drift from the land which continued during this period would offset any tendency to an increase. Large numbers of agricultural labourers were leaving the land to work in the industrial areas, or on railway construction, or else to emigrate.

[2] "In 1740 the population was 15,000, in 1847 it was 82,340, almost as large as it is at the present time." G. F. Vale, *Old Bethnal Green* (1934), p. 23.

11

necessary to go to the Parish Registers, which from 1812 onwards give particulars as to the " Quality, Trade or Profession " of the fathers of the children baptised. The most numerous group is the agricultural labourers, styled "husbandmen " in the registers. Then we have the men of quality—the gentlemen, esquires, merchants, etc., and the servants of their households—the gardeners, coachmen, grooms, butlers, valets, maids, and charwomen. We have the group of copper-workers already mentioned, and a few people outside these categories, amongst whom may be mentioned a mantua-maker, a barge-builder, a meat-salesman, a soap-boiler, a looking-glass frame-maker, and significantly if we remember present-day Walthamstow, one office clerk, and one " engeneer."

Finally, we have the shop-keepers and others ministering to the needs of this population,—to mention a few, butcher, baker, grocer, cornchandler, tallow chandler, shoemaker, cheesemonger, hairdresser, taylor, optician, chimney sweep, coal merchant, greengrocer, linen draper, fishmonger, upholsterer, oilman and watchmaker. In addition to these tradesmen, the following are mentioned— surgeon, schoolmaster, letter-carrier, bricklayer, carpenter, wheelwright, painter, plumber, publican, millwright, carrier, horsekeeper, harness-maker, hostler, sawyer, mason, tinman. These details, which are, of course, by no means complete, are taken from an analysis of the Baptismal Registers between the years 1812 and 1837.

So much for the occupations of the local population a hundred years ago. What were the conditions of life, and how did this community govern itself ? We must remember that at this time the population of Walthamstow fell into three fairly clearly defined groups—the very

12

wealthy occupants of the big houses, the "respectable tradesmen," and the labouring class, always very close to poverty.

During the eighteenth century, great changes affected the rural population. The Agricultural Revolution, heralded by the work of such men as "Turnip" Townshend, and other pioneers of improved crop rotation and mixed farming, gave the death blow to the old system of cultivation, and converted the former sturdy yeomanry of England into the landless agricultural labourers of the early nineteenth century. Round London, very advanced methods of agriculture were introduced early in the eighteenth century, chiefly by the milk-producers, graziers, and nursery gardeners. And so it seems that in these districts enclosures took place very early. Clarke, in his " *Walthamstow, Past, Present and Future* " (1861) states that in 1746 the 4,320 acres of the parish were made up as follows : 3,000 acres enclosed, 350 acres open field, and the rest woodland, roads, and forest waste. And of the 350 acres of open field, over 200 acres were comprised in the three parish commons.

The plight of the people who worked on the land, always difficult, became desperate at the end of the eighteenth century. The manifold changes effected by the Industrial and Agricultural Revolutions ensured high prices for agricultural produce, but wages lagged very far behind, and a bad harvest or other calamity threw the the labourers and their families on the mercy of the parish.

But despite these great changes, the old machinery of local government, creaking in many places, still continued in service. In Walthamstow, as in other parishes, government in the early nineteenth century was by the

Vestry ; its officers, the Churchwarden, the Overseer of the Poor and the Surveyor of Highways ; and its servants, the Beadle, the Master of the Workhouse, the Constable and the Vestry Clerk.

The most important department of local government in the early nineteenth century was undoubtedly that concerned with the relief of the poor. Adequate treatment of this subject is impossible here, but it is necessary to outline the main aspects of poor relief as it affected our parish. Since Elizabethan times, the whole trend of poor-law legislation had been to make the relief of the poor the especial duty of the parish in which they could prove settlement. As the administration of poor relief was in the hands of representatives of the larger rate-payers of the district, economy was the keynote, and relief was given only to those whose plight was really desperate. In 1722, an Act was passed empowering those parishes which possessed Workhouses to refuse out-door relief to all who refused to be "lodged, kept or maintained there." This meant more economy, and it was no doubt under this Act that Walthamstow's Parish Workhouse was built.

But the widespread pauperization towards the end of the eighteenth century necessitated a revision of the strict controls of the Elizabethan Poor Law system. In 1795, the Poor Relief Act was passed, sanctioning the giving of relief in the poor person's home, and authorising justices to give orders for poor relief. In the same year, the Berkshire magistrates meeting at Speenhamland, in view of the hardship caused by low rates of pay, recommended not that the pay should be raised, but that an allowance should be paid in aid of wages out of the poor

14

rates in proportion to the price of bread, and the size of the family. This device was widely adopted, and the result was to bring nearly all the labourers on the land within the shadow of poor relief.

Unfortunately, we have no Vestry Minutes for the early nineteenth century, so that a clear picture of the working of poor relief in this parish could only be gained from a detailed analysis of the Overseers' Vouchers and such records as have survived. But there is good reason to believe that the distress in the parish was mitigated by two factors (i) the opportunities of seasonal labour on the big estates and elsewhere, and (ii) the operation of quite considerable charities which were administered in Walthamstow.

In view of the widespread distress, and the practical certainty that old age, sickness or unemployment would necessitate recourse to " the Parish," poor people looked very carefully to their legal settlement which gave them the right to claim assistance or a place in the workhouse. But the Overseers were just as anxious to prove that a pauper had no legal settlement in their parish, and to demand his removal to another parish. We have many examples of the harsh way in which poor people were hustled out of the parish lest they should become a burden on the rates in the Walthamstow Vestry Minutes of the eighteenth century,[1] for example, in 1759, " Paid to get rid of Mr. Suttons servant she being big with child £1 1s. 0d."

For the early part of the nineteenth century, we have

---

[1] S. J. Barns, *Walthamstow Vestry Minutes, Churchwardens' and Overseers' Accounts*, 1710–1794. (W.A.S. 13, 14 and 16).

a book recording the examinations of paupers,[1] of which the following, dated 15 Feb. 1823, is typical :

" The examination of James Gray now residing in the parish of Walthamstow in the said County, and chargeable thereto, taken upon oath touching the place of his last legal settlement.

"Who saith he is of the age of Seventy Two and was born in the parish of Great Wishford in the County of Wilts. That about Forty nine Years ago, he let himself as a yearly servant to Mr. Thomas Mowdry of Great Wishford in the County aforesaid at the wages of five pounds per annum, board and lodging, and lived with his master Two Years under that hiring, that he was never married nor done any act whereby to gain a subsequent settlement. Sworn this 15 day of February 1823. Before W.M. Raikes, S. Bosanquet."

Where it could be proved that the place of legal settlement of the pauper was elsewhere, an order was made out by two Justices of the Peace empowering the Churchwardens and Overseers to remove the pauper. Copies of these removal orders, mostly of Walthamstow people sent away from other parishes, are preserved amongst the Overseers' Records.[2] But sometimes the other parish would deny that the pauper had any right of legal settlement there, and then costly litigation would ensue.

Another way in which the Overseer sought the aid of the Magistrates in an endeavour to keep down the cost of poor relief was in respect of illegitimate children. Illegitimacy seems to have been of common occurrence,

---

[1] Examinations concerning Legal Settlements, 1817-1823. P.R. 226.
[2] P.R.

and we have preserved with the Removal Orders several Bastardy Warrants, taken out on the examination of the mothers of these children, enforcing the payment of certain sums by the parents to the parish in return for its care of the children. Naturally, great efforts were made to "apprehend the putative father," to use the language of the warrants, and sometimes the parish put pressure on the parents to marry.

The fate of the parish children can be guessed at. Life in the workhouse was hard enough, but as soon as they were old enough, the parish got rid of them by apprenticing them for a sum down to anybody who would have them. Sometimes there were safeguards, but often the children were looked upon as mere slaves, and were not taught any trade. In the Walthamstow Register of Parish Apprentices, 1819-1837,[1] we find them bound to the following—farrier, fisherman, miller, ropemaker, shoemaker and taylor. Other trades are mentioned, but none were bound to chimney-sweeps.

And here, at the risk of a digression, I should like to mention the part played by this parish in the movement against the inhuman method of chimney-sweeping common in the early nineteenth century. We are told that there was a flue in Walthamstow Parish Church which was so difficult to clean that the chimney-boy had to enter it head-first.[2] And in *The Chimney-Sweeper's Friend and Climbing Boy's Album*, published in 1824, we read the following case : " In the beginning of the year 1808, a chimney-sweeper's boy being employed to sweep a chimney in Marsh Street, Walthamstow, in the house

---

[1] P.R. 45.

[2] V. Cohen, *The Nineteenth Century* (1932), p. 165.

17

of Mr. Jeffery, carpenter, unfortunately in his attempt to get down, stuck in the flue, and was unable to extricate himself. Mrs. Jeffery, being within hearing of the boy, immediately procured assistance. As the chimney was low, and the top of it easily accessible from without, the boy was taken out in about ten minutes, the chimney-pot and several rows of bricks having been previously removed. If he had remained in that dreadful situation many minutes longer, he must have died. His master was sent for, and he arrived soon after the boy had been released. He abused him for the accident, and after striking him, sent him with a bag of soot to sweep another chimney. The child appeared so very weak when taken out that he could scarcely stand, and yet this wretched being, who had been up ever since three o'clock, had before been sent by his master to Wanstead, which, with his walk to Marsh Street, made about 5 miles." This, incidentally, is one of the mildest cases recorded.

But there were people in Walthamstow who were determined to put a stop to these horrors, and members of the Forster family of Hale End and a Wigram served on the Committee of a " Society for superseding the Necessity of Climbing Boys by encouraging a New Method of Sweeping Chimneys . . .¹ It was probably owing to the activities of these gentlemen that in 1816 a meeting of the inhabitants of Walthamstow and Leyton, convened by the vicars of the two parishes, passed resolutions urging that measures should be taken immediately in Walthamstow and Leyton to promote the use of machines for chimney sweeping " in consideration of the various complicated miseries to which children are

¹ *The Chimney-Sweeper's Friend, etc.*

1. Parish church of St. Mary, Walthamstow, as illustrated in Ogbourne's *History of Essex*, 1814. It was later altered and enlarged.

2. Highams in 1800. Built in 1768 by Jeremiah Harman, the house is now the central part of Woodford High School for Girls. The grounds and Highams Park Lake were laid out by Humphrey Repton.

3. Walthamstow House in Shernhall Street was rebuilt in 1782 by Robert Wigram, M.P. for Fowey in Cornwall 1802-06. In 1885 it became St. Mary's orphanage and is in use today for education and religious purposes.

4. Grosvenor House, Hoe Street in 1792. A modern school is on the site now. Rebuilt in the late 18th century by Field Marshal Grosvenor, re-fronted by William Selwyn, it became a trade school in 1897 and eventually was destroyed by fire.

5. Belle Vue House estate was bounded by Forest Road, Hale End Road and the forest. The early 19th century house was built by Charles Cook, publisher, who died in 1816. The estate was sold for housing in 1899.

6. Ferry Bridge. This wooden structure was built in 1760 across the river Lea beside the Ferry Boat Inn by Sir William Maynard, lord of the manor of Walthamstow Toni. It was demolished in 1915.

7. The Eagle pond and inn at Snaresbrook in 1819. The boundary of Walthamstow extends to the foreground of the picture.

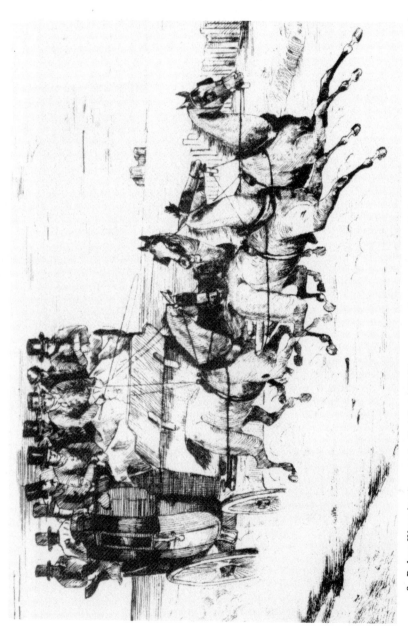

8. Robert Wragg's stage coach plied from Walthamstow to the City before Lea Bridge Station was opened in 1840. A drawing by Thomas Moxon of Leyton, c.1838.

liable who are employed to sweep chimneys," and that a subscription should be opened to promote endeavours to abolish the practice of employing children in these parishes[1].

But to return to the activities of the Overseer of the Poor in this parish. Space does not allow a careful analysis of the surviving Overseers' Records. Briefly, we find that the money collected on the Poor Rate went to pay the Workhouse Expenses, Outdoor Relief, expenses of poor people in Hospitals and Lunatic Asylums, the salaries of the Parish Officers, the County Rate, and other incidental expenses, amongst which dinners on auspicious occasions loom large. Naturally, the administration of the Workhouse was one of the Overseers' main duties, and by good fortune a copy of the printed " Rules and Regulations to be observed in, and relating to the Workhouse " made at a Vestry in September, 1830, has come down to us[2].

On entering the Workhouse, each man and boy was provided with a coat, waistcoat and hat, two pairs of drab coloured fustian small clothes, two pairs of mixed colour worsted stockings, two shirts, a pair of shoes, two neckerchiefs, and two pocket handkerchiefs. Each woman was to be provided with two shifts, two flannel petticoats, one stuff petticoat, one stuff gown, two aprons, two handkerchiefs, two pocket handkerchiefs, two pair of black worsted stockings, three caps and a pair of shoes.

The diet was quite simple—for Breakfast, milk porridge every morning; for Dinner, Sunday, boiled beef, Monday, pease soup, Tuesday, beef or mutton, Wednesday, soup,

---

[1] W.C. 806.

[2] Workhouse Committee : Minutes, 1834-5. P.R. 59.

Thursday, boiled beef or mutton, Friday, pease soup, Saturday, cold meat and bread and cheese ; and for Supper, bread and cheese every night. "And of beer each man and woman is to have a pint, and each child half a pint at dinner, and the same quantities at supper, and on Christmas Day, Easter Day and Whitsunday, for dinner, Roast Beef and Plumb Pudding and an extra pint of porter to be allowed to each man and woman, and half a pint to each child." "All the paupers in health, including children above seven years of age, during such time as they are not sent to school, are to be employed in work suitable to their strength and condition." They are all to attend Divine Service in a group every Lords-day, but "they are to be seated in good time before the service is begun, and to stay until the congregation be departed." There are many other rules, mostly concerned with the good behaviour of the inmates.

From the minutes of a Committee,[1] formed to assist the Overseers, it appears that the number of paupers in the Workhouse was about 80, that the inmates were employed in picking oakum, and that beer was brewed on the premises. Discipline was strict, and one unfortunate, Sarah Plummer, was kept in solitary confinement on a bread and water diet for a week for some misdemeanour. One resolution of the Committee directs that able-bodied paupers, presumably on outdoor relief, are to be employed digging and wheeling gravel for the Surveyor, but the allowance given is to be considerably less than the ordinary wages given for similar work to independent labourers. The gravel is to be wheeled in

---

[1] P.R. 59.

20

barrows on the roads, each barrow containing a bushel, and the distance traversed to be not less than 16 miles a day! The time of daily work is to be from daybreak to dark, one hour being allowed for dinner.

At this period, poor relief varied tremendously from parish to parish. In 1834 a new Poor Law Act was passed which aimed at creating some uniformity, and as a result this parish was banded together with others in the West Ham Union. A new workhouse was established to serve the area, and in 1836, Walthamstow Workhouse ceased to exist. From then on, the Overseers lost a certain measure of their importance and functions in this locality.

The activities of the Churchwarden and the Surveyor of the Highways may be passed over here. By this time, the Churchwarden had lost much of his status as a secular officer, and the Churchwardens' Accounts that have survived deal mainly with routine Church matters. Similarly, the Surveyors' Accounts have none of that interest for us which the Overseers' Records possess. But there is one other aspect of local government in these days which needs consideration—the policing of the parish.

Before the establishment of a regular police force by Sir Robert Peel, the problem in a parish such as this was a difficult one. Despite the savage sentences of public execution and transportation which were passed on wrongdoers, crime was rife, and the big houses in these unlighted country lanes were tempting prey. The one or two old men appointed as parish constables were completely ineffective, and in 1819 it was decided to set up a Patrol and Watch Committee "for the purpose of

21

establishing a more efficient Police in this Parish."[1] The Committee was financed by voluntary subscriptions, and the force it administered consisted of one Head Horse Patrol at 35 shillings per week, one under Horse Patrol at 30 shillings per week, and eight Foot Patrols at 14 shillings per week. Pistols were issued to the men, but were only to be used in the most urgent case of self-defence.

The Minutes of this Committee are full of interest. The patrols do not seem to have been very conscientious, and at one meeting Penn, the Superintendent, reported that " Henry Stevens had slept on duty, and call'd the hour wrong two or three times, and finally, while asleep, Penn took away his Cutlass. He was call'd in and discharg'd by the Committee as a man incompetent to the duty."

Penn seems to have been fairly active, and in Oct. 1821 reports that he had arrested a certain William Brewer at the bottom of Marsh Street near Mr. Warner's corner for insulting behaviour, but Brewer " escaped on Sunday Afternoon between 3 and 4 O'clock by sawing through the lining of the Cage, and forcing out the Brickwork of the wall nine inch in thickness." Another patrol testified as to Brewer's threatening language, and told of Brewer " snapping his fingers, and saying he would as lief kill him (meaning as they supposed Penn) as eat his Victuals, that he was the fattest of the three and ought to be kill'd first."

A fortnight later, Penn reports that hearing a disturbance at one o'clock in the morning in Marsh Street, he

---

[1] Police Committee : Minutes and Accounts, 1819–1822. P.R. 61.

went out and advised the men concerned to go home. But as he was returning to his house, a pistol was fired, and James Brewer (brother to William) shouted " Now is your time, we are True Britons, come on, we are prepared to meet the whole set." Penn continues " He then ran across the road to my house. Saying We will have the Master of the gang first, putting himself in a fighting attitude, and telling me to bring up my whole troop, they were armed as well as we and prepared to meet them. He said we had imprisoned his Brother, but should not (have) him, he would suffer himself to be cut into Mince Meat first." It was reported that James Brewer had been apprehended, and William Brewer committed to Barking Jail.

In 1831, a new Committee[1] was set up under an " Act to make Provision for the Lighting and Watching of Parishes in England and Wales," passed in 1830. This Act gave power to levy a rate, and under it the position of the Committee was regularised. Robert Maynard was appointed Superintendent of the Police at 21 shillings per week, and eight patrols were appointed at 15 shillings per week. One of the first cases recorded was against Mr. Shaddrick of the Royal Oak, a public house which used to stand in College Place, on the forest. The policeman reported " hearing a loud talking as if quarelling at ½ past 11 o'clock; he knocked at the door and on the second knock a female voice answered who is there, on which he answered Police, and heard immediately a a skuffle as though persons were moving out of the back door..." He ran round to the back and caught the

---

[1] Lighting and Watching Committee : Minute Book, 1831-1840. P.R. 64.

roysterers, and after a fight, arrested two. But the magistrate dismissed the charges, and an indignant letter to the Home Secretary brought no results.

The Committee continued to have difficulties with the men in its employ, and in February 1832, the charge was brought against the Sergeant, a man named Perks at this time, that he had been drunk at the Duke's Head in Wood Street when he should have been on his beat. The Committee decided to discharge him, and ordered him to give up his police clothing. This he refused to do, and we are told that the Committee had to direct that it might be taken from him, " which was only done after the most gross and violent behaviour on his part."

In 1840, the Metropolitan Police took over the policing of this parish, and its independent system came to an end. The new system may have been more efficient, but it cannot have been more picturesque than the one it displaced.

To conclude this sketch of local government, it may be useful to indicate the amount of the rates at this period. A note[1] left on people who were out when the rate-collector called, dated 1832, show the amounts levied as 2s. 9d. in the £ for the Poor Rate, 6d. in the £ for the Church Rate, and 4½d. in the £ on houses and 1½d. in the £ on land for the Police Rate, making a total rate of 3s. 6d. in the £.

The charities available in the parish are set out fully in an interesting little booklet issued by the vicar in 1840. It is entitled " A Manual of Useful Information for Residents in the Parish of Walthamstow respecting the

---

[1] Overseers' Vouchers, 1832. P.R.

Institutions, Benefactions, Charities, and other matters of Religious and General Interest in the Parish, intended more especially for the Poor, to assist those of good character and prudent habits to better their condition,.... by William Wilson, B.D., Vicar." In his introduction, Wilson is very careful to impress on his readers the necessity for self-help, for "Long observation has sufficiently convinced him, that few things are so calculated, secretly, gradually, but surely, to poison the sources of morality and religion in a neighbourhood, as indiscrimate and reckless charity," whilst on the other hand "Self-cultivation, honest industry, prudence, sobriety, and, above all, truly religious habits, if they do not lead to a competency, will, at least, while they secure the respect of all around, raise them above those extreme wants which sometimes attend a state of poverty."

The Manual informs us that £696 was available annually from local charities. Particulars are given of the local almshouses, and of the following local societies: Benefit Society, Benevolent Society, Bible Association, Cheap Clothing Society, Children's Shoe Society, Coal Club, Female Benefit Society, Friendly Sick Society, Lying-in Charity and the Spade Husbandry Society. Educational facilities, other than the private academies, are listed: Boys' and Girls' National Schools, District Infant Schools and the Monoux School ("The charge upon each pupil, who enjoys the benefit of the foundation is ten shillings per quarter, to be paid in advance. This sum includes every expense except that for printed books. There are at present (1839) in the Monoux School twenty-three boys, of whom nineteen are upon the foundation.")

Two libraries are mentioned, a Parochial Lending Library, kept in the Robing Room at the Church, consisting of " religious, useful and entertaining books," and a Sunday Library of " books suitable for Sunday reading." In addition, facilities are mentioned for obtaining Bibles, Prayer Books and Hymn Books cheaply or free of charge. Finally, Wilson gives particulars of the Leyton Savings' Bank, of local church accommodation and services, and of pasturage rights on the local commons, marshes and forest. It will be seen that the facilities available in Walthamstow were quite considerable, bearing in mind the period, and must, I imagine, have compared favourably with those in other districts.[1]

Religious developments at this time have been dealt with fully in the Antiquarian Society's monographs, and so far as the Nonconformists are concerned, in H. D. Budden's *Story of Marsh Street Congregational Church, Walthamstow*, 1923. It will merely be necessary, then, to recall the salient points here.

At the beginning of the century, the vicar at St. Mary's, the Rev. Edward Conyers, was a pluralist who was also vicar of Epping, and lived at Copt Hall, Epping. Most of the duties fell on the curate, William Sparrow, who lived at the Vicarage, and is buried in the parish church. During this period, pressure on space is indicated by the constant applications for pews and accommodation for servants preserved in the Churchwardens' Records. The population was growing, and the church had to grow too, though unfortunately it had to

---

[1] But for a criticism of friendly societies at this period, see Dr. W. Hasbach, *A History of the English Agricultural Labourer* (1920), p. 233.

grow at a time when regard for beautiful and historical buildings was practically non-existent. The details of the transformation which overtook the parish church have been recounted elsewhere[1], but the extent of the change is best seen in the prints and pictures in the Walthamstow Museum. In the prints about 1800 we see an interesting building with a red brick tower, a clerestoried nave, a chancel with five light window, a low south aisle and a small north aisle ending in the Monoux chapel. In prints of the mid-nineteenth century, we see the standardized and practically rebuilt building covered in drab cement, which we know today.

The main alterations took place in 1806, 1818 and then in 1843, when the Church was in the hands of the Rev. William Wilson, who succeeded Conyers in 1822. But soon it had to be recognized that one church could no longer serve the needs of the whole parish, and three daughter churches were erected—St. John's, built 1839-40, St. Peter's, built 1840, and St. James', built 1841-2. All the money for these churches, which cost £6,500, was raised by subscription, except for a grant of £250.[2] St. John's and St. James' have since been rebuilt, though many people in Walthamstow must remember the original churches. St. Peter's is the original building.

The Nonconformists have always had quite a vigorous community in Walthamstow, drawing their strength in the early years from London merchant families, like the Cowards and Sollys, resident in Walthamstow. At the beginning of the nineteenth century there were two

---

[1] G. F. Bosworth, *A History of St. Mary's Church, Walthamstow* (W.A.S. 2).

[2] *Walthamstow, Past, Present and Future*, p. 20.

Chapels in Marsh Street. One, the old Meeting House as it was called, stood on the site of the present Marsh Street Congregational Church, and inclined to Unitarian doctrine. Through the instrumentality of Henry Solly, Eliezer Cogan came here as Minister in 1801, and in the end of the year established his school at Essex Hall.

The other chapel, the present Methodist Chapel in High Street, was known as the New Meeting House. Collison was minister from 1797 to 1837, and was succeeded by Joseph Freeman. It was Freeman who linked Walthamstow with the missionary efforts of the time. Through him, the Malagasy refugees were brought to Walthamstow, and a " School for the Daughters of Missionaries "[1] was established here in 1838, which was so successful that in 1841 another " Home and School for the Sons and Orphans of Missionaries " was founded here. The Old Meeting House had been closed about 1830 for lack of support, but in 1811 a small chapel had been built in Wood Street under the direction of people from the New Meeting House.

Education locally in the early nineteenth century was largely under the auspices of the Churches. The National School, Church End, was established in 1819 from St. Mary's Church, and others were founded in conjunction with the new Churches. Then there was the Nonconformist British School in Marsh Street, and the Infants' School established in the Churchyard in 1828, by the vicar, the Rev. William Wilson. This school, the oldest Church Infants' School in the country, had been carried on previously in a barn in Church End, behind the

---

[1] For an account of this school and its subsequent development, see C. E. Curryer, *The Story of Walthamstow Hall* (1938).

National Schools, and had furnished material for an important work by Wilson, *The System of Infants' Schools*, published in 1825. At most of these schools there was a small fee charged, and they were intended for poorer children. But education was not compulsory, child labour was the rule, and illiteracy was widespread.

In addition, the parish abounded at this time with "Academies for the Sons and Daughters of Gentlemen." Prominent amongst these were Cogan's Academy at Essex Hall,[1] with Disraeli as pupil, Dr. Niblock's School at The Priory,[2] Dr. Guy's School[3] (The Forest School) founded in 1834, Dr. Glennie Greig's School at Walthamstow House,[4] and Stephen Eardley's Paradise House Academy already referred to. Amongst the schools for girls, mention should be made of Miss Caley's Boarding School in Marsh Street, attended by Fanny Keats, the sister of the poet John Keats, who lived with her guardians, the Abbeys, further down the street.[5] All these associations have been dealt with elsewhere.

But no account of education in early nineteenth century Walthamstow can omit reference to a passage in the late Rev. E. L. Berthon's *A Retrospect of Eight Decades* (1899). Mr. Berthon, who distinguished himself as an inventor in later life, went to school at the Monoux Grammar School, and tells of his experiences in the following extract (pp. 5-9) :

---

[1] G. F. Bosworth, *Essex Hall, Walthamstow, and the Cogan Associations* (W.A.S. 5).

[2] G. F. Bosworth, *More Walthamstow Houses* (W.A.S. 20), p. 26.

[3] G. F. Bosworth, *Some Walthamstow Houses* (W.A.S. 12), p. 39.

[4] *ibid.*, p. 6.

[5] The Keats' association with Walthamstow is treated very fully in Marie Adami's *Fanny Keats* (1937).

"But oh! that winter, 1819-20, with its 13 weeks' frost, when an ox was roasted whole on the Thames! How we suffered from the bitter cold! We had some fun, though, for the boys made a sledge big enough to carry a dozen. This was drawn by about 50 of us on the frozen roads and the Eagle Pond at Snaresbrook.

"Falling ill, I was sent home; and on regaining strength was despatched to another school kept by a Mr. Roberts. This was supposed to be an improvemeut on the former one, and there were actually basins and jugs in the bedrooms, but in all other respects it was worse.[1] It was in the Churchyard of Walthamstow. Over a long line of almshouses, built before the Reformation, was a wretched drafty loft, with a high-pitched, open-tiled roof; this was our school-room. There had once been a large fireplace at one end, but coals were dear, and the old grate had been replaced by a little one, just big enough to keep Mr. Roberts' toes fairly warm. Over the fireplace was a curious board nearly three hundred years old. It was ten feet long, and bore an inscription recording the name of the founder, "Georgius Monoux hanc scholam fundavit, A.D. 1527."[2]...Every Saturday (for dinner) a large lump of salt beef was brought in, and an iron dish of potatoes, preceded by another, containing what was called by the master "pudding" but by us "stickjaw." Hard as the beef was on Saturday, it was harder still when cold on Sunday. Being very durable, it appeared as the only

---

[1] The boys boarded at Mr. Roberts' house, going across to the Monoux Schoolroom for their lessons. The Rev. J. F. Roberts was curate of Walthamstow at the time, and lived at The Chestnuts, Church Lane. See G. F. Bosworth, *More Walthamstow Houses* (W.A.S. 12), p. 11.

[2] This board is preserved in the library of the present Monoux Grammar School.

meat till Saturday came round again, when the beautifully simple course was renewed. What wonder if we grew weak and ill. I suffered so frightfully with boils all over me, that I was glad to be able to sleep by rolling up my socks into what sailors call a "grummet" and putting the rings round the boils on one side. I think we only lived by spending our pocket money on penny rolls, cheese, treacle, red herrings, and eggs......

"If our dinners were bad our other meals were no better. Hunches of stale bread, with an almost invisible scrape of butter on one of their six sides, were our only food, morning and evening, washed down with milk and water. The order should have been reversed, for it was three parts water to one of milk. We never were so wild or unreasonable as to expect tea or coffee, the former being then about eight shillings a pound, and the latter a luxury for the rich. As for cocoa or chocolate, I don't think they were known in those days.

"One day the mistress overheard the wicked cries of "Sky-blue;" so to put an end to such monstrous audacity, she sailed majestically into the room, when we were at our so-called *Tea*. Unfolding a bill half a yard long, and striking an attitude (which was a bad copy of the then famous actress, Mrs. Siddons) she explained "See here, you ungrateful boys, *nineteen pounds, fifteen shillings* for milk in one year! How dare you talk of sky-blue!" She omitted to say that her large family and her servants had consumed by far the greater part of the fluid. But "the worm will turn"; and as there was no turning in the milky way, we determined upon revenge. So the night before breaking-up we all set to work and smashed every bit of crockery (there were basins in these bedrooms, you remember) that we could lay hands on; and a jolly night we had, singing " Dulce domum " in the wreckage.

" The next morning, the school bell rang; and instead of going home, we were driven across the Churchyard, to see once more the hated inscription, " Georgius Monoux " etc. Old Bob came in black as thunder, followed by a man carrying a brace of most exquisitely constructed birch rods that ever graced the hand of a pedagogue. " No Holidays! I'll flog the lot of you! First class strip." But when he looked upon half-a-dozen big fellows, quite ready for a shindy, he began to hesitate. He then declared he would flog the ringleaders, who were commanded to stand forth. Of course, no one volunteered for the honour. At last a happy thought struck him— we should all draw lots, and the two who got the prizes should take them out in four-and-twenty cuts of those lovely rods.

" Now the two smallest boys in the school were my cousin Ben and myself; both eight years old, having been born on the the same day.[1] How anxiously we watched the faces of the boys, as they drew their lots, beginning with the eldest, and so down. Smiles of relief abounded as one after the other they drew a blank. But at last the bag came to us, with only two lots in it, and on opening the folded papers, we read : " To be flogged." How we blubbered, repeating what we had heard the elder ones say : " Didn't do it with any malicious intent, sir." Old Bob commanded us to strip, but at the sight of our wretched little skinny backs, his fury seemed to leak out; and after a few whisks of the rod in his hand, and the

---

[1] This fixes the date of these happenings at the Monoux School as 1821.

pretty music it made in the air, he threw it down saying "There, go home! I'll pay you off next half." So happily ended the only rebellion in which I ever took part."

The Rev. E. L. Berthon's reminiscences throw many interesting sidelights on life at this period. He tells of the inconvenience of the days before the use of lucifer matches, when the tinder box had to be relied upon, and when theatres were illuminated by dips and rushlights. He tells of a visit to the pantomime, to see the famous Grimaldi, of the appearance of the Shillibeer omnibus, and whalebone parasols. He tells us of his excitement at seeing the first passenger steamer on the Thames in 1822, and he tells us, too, that in the days before Sir Robert Peel, when "wheezy old "Charlies" with their rattles and watchboxes" did police duty, many of the big houses in this district had their own watchmen. Highway robberies were common, and one night when Berthon's father was coming home along the Lea Bridge Road with his cousin, Sir Edward Barnes, a gallant general who had been made a G.C.B. for his bravery at Waterloo, they were held up at the pistol's point, and relieved of their watches and purses. But subsequently the highwayman was captured, and it was found that the pistol which had inspired such fear was only the stem of a brass candlestick.[1]

Organised games in the early nineteenth century were the exception rather than the rule, so that the following solitary reference, in a cutting from a contemporary newspaper, to a cricket match played at Walthamstow in 1816, is worth quoting :

"A grand match at Cricket was played at Waltham-

---

[1] E. L. Berthon's *Retrospect*, pp. 14-15.

stow, on Thursday the 22nd inst. between the Walthamstow Club and the *Strength of Enfield*. This match was so ably contested, that the night alone obliged them to give in and meet again the following Monday for the purpose of finishing the game. It was then won in a spirited and masterly manner by the Walthamstow Club, beating their opponents by 42 runs. This match had been for some time the topic of conversation, and many bets were depending—consequently it attracted a great concourse of spectators, among whom were Lord Viscount Maynard, and many others of the neighbouring gentry."[1]

In the big houses which abounded in Walthamstow at this period a number of interesting people were living, but the houses and their occupants have all been fully treated elsewhere.[2] But we must not forget that this period saw the birth of Walthamstow's greatest son, William Morris, in a house on Clay Hill which has disappeared so completely that the only record we have of it is one rather unsatisfactory pen-sketch. Morris's father, whose fine tomb may be seen in Woodford churchyard, was in many ways typical of the new-rich people of these years. A lucky investment built a fortune which enabled the family to move to a fine estate at Woodford Hall, and ensured sufficient affluence to allow William Morris to follow his artistic interests later on. Mr. Morris senior does not seem to have been very popular as the new master at Woodford Hall, and in " *Paul Pry*," a scandal-mongering paper of the time, we read the following : " We advise the far-famed ex-auctioneer W. Morris, of

---

[1] W.C. 807.

[2] See Mr. Bosworth's Monographs on the Old Houses of Walthamstow (W.A.S. 12, 20 and 29).

Woodford Hall, not to be so uncharitable as to try to prevent poor people from getting water, this severe weather, from off his premises."[1]

There are several cuttings from this paper, of 1840 date, at the Walthamstow Museum referring to Walthamstow people, and I cannot resist quoting one or two extracts. The law of libel must have been very weak when such items as these could be published : " Why does Miss May wear a cabbage net when she comes to Hale End ; is it to keep the wind from off her beautiful face, or is it to make people believe that there is more under it than it would be prudent to expose."[2]

" Bo-peep wishes to know if Miss Charlotte Wright has recovered from the dreadful fall from Mr. Wragg's coach coming from town. We are surprised that you cannot find a protector. Drink moderately, and learn to moderate your amiable temper, Miss, and we hope some-one will take compassion."[3]

Then one about Wragg himself : " There is no harm in Wragg, the coachmaster, starting an omnibus, if he did not interfere with the time of a poor widow, who has a far greater right on the road than he has. He should recollect that he will ultimately be a loser, by thus endeavouring to oppress and ruin a widow, who has no other means of subsistence than the profits of the coach he is now hoping to run off the road. Reform, and be satisfied with what you have, or we shall let out more than will be pleasant, old cock."[4]

We do not know what happened to the widow's coach, but Wragg's coach certainly prospered, and ran from the Nag's Head to Bishopsgate regularly for many years to

---

[1] W.C. 1653.   [2] *ibid.* 854.   [3] *ibid.* 852.   [4] *ibid.* 839.

come. And this reminder of a time when the only
method of travel to London was by coach, on horseback
or on foot, prompts us, before concluding, to a final
glance at the Walthamstow of a hundred years ago.
Roads were poor, travel difficult and amusements few.
But the parish, well-wooded and hilly, must have been a
beautiful place to live in. The shops and main centres of
population were in Marsh Street and Wood Street,
and there were a number of hamlets or "Ends" at
Church End, Hale End, Chapel End, King's End (in the
"Slip"), Clay Street, Higham Hill and Forest Rise.[1]
The rest of the parish, apart from the forest and the
marshes, was either under cultivation, or divided among
the estates of the big houses. In addition, there were
three fine commons—Church Common, Higham Hill
Common, and Markhouse Common,—which the parish-
oners had managed to preserve until they were finally
enclosed in 1848[2].

Externally, at any rate, Walthamstow of 1850 cannot
have differed very considerably from the Walthamstow of
1650. But change was soon to overwhelm the place. A
station of the Eastern Counties Railway had been opened
at Lea Bridge in 1840, sewers, gas lighting and a water
supply soon followed. Between 1851 and 1861 the
population increased from 4,959 to 7,144, an increase
foreshadowing the great influx that was to take place with
the introduction of the railway and cheap fares into
Walthamstow. Within a few decades the main features
of the Walthamstow we know today were fixed.

---

[1] For the topography of the parish at this period, the fine map of
1822, executed by John Coe, the Vestry Clerk, is invaluable. E.C. 358.

[2] The opposition of the parishioners in 1828 compelled the with-
drawal of a previous Enclosure proposal. E.C. 170.